For the souls who will inherit the earth from us,
and for the ones who didn't make it here.
H. N. K.

For my wonderful nephews, Louie and Freddie.
R. D.

First published 2022 by Macmillan Children's Books
an imprint of Pan Macmillan
The Smithson, 6 Briset Street, London EC1M 5NR
EU representative: Macmillan Publishers Ireland Ltd,
1st Floor, The Liffey Trust Centre,
117–126 Sheriff Street Upper, Dublin 1, D01 YC43
Associated companies throughout the world
www.panmacmillan.com

ISBN 978-1-5290-5307-4

Text copyright © Hiba Noor Khan 2022
Illustrations copyright © Rachael Dean 2022

The right of Hiba Noor Khan and Rachael Dean to be identified as the
author and illustrator of this work has been asserted by them in accordance
with the Copyright, Designs and Patents Act 1988.

1 3 5 7 9 8 6 4 2

A CIP catalogue record for this book is available from the British Library.

Design and reuse artworking by Susannah Mason

Printed and bound in China

HIBA NOOR KHAN

ONE HOME

ILLUSTRATED BY
RACHAEL DEAN

MACMILLAN CHILDREN'S BOOKS

CONTENTS

Introduction   5

Amelia Telford   6

Catalina Silva   10

Aditya Mukarji   14

Blue Sandford   18

India Logan-Riley   22

Lina Yassin   26

Ellen-Anne   30

Sumak Helena Gualinga   34

Litokne Kabua   38

Emaan Danish Khan   42

Genevieve Leroux   46

Kim Yu-Jin   50

Remy Zahiga   54

Sophia Kianni   58

Swietenia Puspa Lestari   62

Yola Mgogwana   66

Makaśa Looking Horse   70

Nikita Shulga   74

Glossary   78

About the Author and Illustrator   80

INTRODUCTION

The natural world has always enchanted and inspired me. My mum and dad filled my childhood with forests and babbling brooks, wildflower meadows and camping by the sea. I was raised to respect and honour the environment, and since then I've been lucky enough to travel across the planet and experience its wonders. Through these journeys, I truly began to understand the threats our world now faces.

I spent time in the Amazon jungle and learnt how enormous areas of precious forest are destroyed every single minute. I was amazed by the wonderful ecosystems around me, but also heartbroken to see how threatened they and their communities now are. While swimming amongst dazzling coral reefs in the Red Sea, I witnessed the destruction that global warming has on sea life. In Tanzania I saw the impacts of deforestation – when trees were burnt down, soil became so dry that no food could be grown in it, forcing people to leave their homes to avoid starvation. From Egypt to Chile, from Pakistan to England, I saw our world changing in worrying ways.

Our planet functions in perfect balance, and we are all joined to each other through it. There are poems in the trees, secrets in the sea and songs in the breezes, but over the centuries most humans have forgotten how to hear them. In losing touch with the world that nourishes and protects us, we've harmed it immensely, ruining its original balance. With animals and plants becoming extinct, sea levels rising fast and climates changing dangerously, things seem desperate, but as nature teaches us, hope is never lost. On the pages of this book you'll meet eighteen inspiring young people who have decided to be the change they wish to see. Just like the powerful, unstoppable wave that forms when lots of drops of water resist and rise together, I have hope in the hearts, voices and actions of young people to change things for the better.

Just as every raindrop, insect and leaf plays a special and important role in their ecosystem, so too do you. There is only one of you, with a unique heart, mind, ideas and skills. Will you join the rising wave, taking your place in the fight for our home?

Hiba Noor Khan

Amelia Telford

BIO

Amelia Telford's home is Tweed Heads, a town south of Brisbane nestled on the Pacific Coast in northern New South Wales, Australia. Amelia is from the Indigenous Bundjalung people, who have called the lush Tweed Valley their home since ancient times. When Amelia saw the impacts of climate change in her country, she decided to give her people a much-needed voice and do what she could to fight it. Indigenous communities around the world are the hardest hit by climate change, but they also have a long history of protecting and defending the land.

Amelia was raised on the coast and grew up visiting the ocean every day. She witnessed the rising sea level changing the coastline, as well as devastating bush fires inland that grew worse every year. Her parents taught her to respect the land that has provided for the Bundjalung for generations, so when she saw climate change affecting it, she turned to activism. Indigenous communities don't just have to fight against the threat of rising sea levels and severe weather, but also the actual destruction of their sacred home. Supported by greedy governments, banks and businesses, fossil fuel industries are able to make money by ruthlessly extracting oil, gas and coal from the land.

Amelia joined youth climate organisations and attended strikes and protests against climate injustice, fighting for the belief that no one's home should be harmed by anyone else's actions. Seeing the thousands of other young people fighting for the planet felt empowering. However, she realised that Indigenous communities were not as represented as the rest of the population, and so she worked hard to set up Australia's first Indigenous youth network; Seed. As the name suggests, something small grew into a powerful movement, and Amelia encouraged young Indigenous people to uphold the important traditions of their ancestors in protecting the planet.

By educating each other on climate issues and embracing differences, Amelia believes that the bullying tactics used by businesses and governments to divide people can be overcome. She enjoys being creative in her campaigning, and once dressed up as Nemo, representing the threatened Great Barrier Reef, to protest outside banks planning to fund a big coal mine. After much pressure from young people around the country, four big banks refused to finance the mine!

HOME

Amelia's home town sits beside the Tweed mountain range, which contains the majestic Wollumbin mountain, one of the many sacred sites for the Bundjalung, where the Tweed River flows through the valley into the ocean. The wider region of New South Wales varies from vibrant rainforests to vast dry outback, from pale sandy beaches to towering mountains.

These varied ecosystems are home to all sorts of wonderful animals, from the endangered Coxen's fig parrot, glossy black cockatoos, humpback whales to bottlenose dolphins and huge turtles. Native little wombats, leaping kangaroos, pygmy possums, fur seals and little penguins also call the region home. Furry koalas, curious platypuses, bandicoots, flying foxes and spiky echidnas can be found along with laughing kookaburras, flightless emus and rare purple copper butterflies.

The Great Barrier Reef lies off the Australian coast and is the world's largest coral reef, one of the most colourful, complex ecosystems on our planet. From manta rays to tiger and whale sharks, seahorses, potato cod, pufferfish, butterflyfish, clownfish and surgeonfish, there are thousands of spectacular species that call the reefs home. Dugongs live alongside colourful jellyfish, dolphins, sea snakes and seven species of sea turtle, supported by the beautiful collection of coral and sea sponges.

Coral reefs are complex, fragile structures that require specific conditions to survive, but climate change has altered these conditions so much that many corals have been left as skeletons, starved and bleached. This has devastating knock-on effects for the rest of the marine life, and over half of the corals have died since 2016. On land, scientists predict that the rising temperatures will increase the amount of bush fires and droughts for Australia, threatening human and animal life.

But there is opportunity too. Australia is very sunny and very windy, making it the perfect place to create renewable energy from the sun and the wind. Together with other young people around the world, Amelia hopes to change the narrative for her people and the planet to a hopeful, harmonious one.

CHALLENGE

Amelia has a strong connection with all elements of her home, from the beaches to the mountains, to the forests. Food can form a big part of our link to the natural world, and when we simply buy everything we eat from a shop, often wrapped in plastic, we can lose this important relationship.

Growing your own food is a wonderful and cost-effective way to to eat organic and pesticide free, which is better for both your body and the planet. Seeing vegetables grow from seeds to their full, nutritious and delicious form gives us an appreciation for the incredible work that the earth does for us each and every day.

Pick somewhere in your home with a bit of room and a lot of light, like an empty windowsill or a sunny corner. Find containers, whether they are plant pots, tins or buckets, and make sure they have a small hole or two in the bottom for water to drain through. Fill them with soil and get planting your seeds or saplings! You'll be able to find these in garden centres or supermarkets. Start with foods that are easy to grow, such as carrots, radishes, strawberries and beans, and make sure you pick appropriately sized containers – carrots will naturally need a deeper pot than mint! Water your garden regularly and find out how best to care for and harvest each plant.

Catalina Silva

BIO

Catalina Silva grew up in a small town called Villa O'Higgins, nestled in the Patagonian Andes mountain range in Chile. Growing up surrounded by dazzling turquoise lakes, huge glaciers and soaring mountains, she developed a deep respect for nature from an early age. Most of her free time was spent in the forests and on the lakes near her home, and her close connection to the environment meant that Catalina saw the effects of climate change first hand.

Lake O'Higgins, located just beside the town, is the deepest lake in South America, and Catalina often sailed on it with her dad when she was young. She was amazed by the dramatic blue-tinged glaciers stretching way into the distance, and first walked on one when she was ten. During each freezing winter Catalina would wade through knee-high snow, but as she got older she noticed that there was less and less snowfall, until it barely happened at all . . . And it wasn't just the weather that was changing – Catalina soon realised that the huge glaciers were shrinking too, melting into their blue lagoons.

As she saw the mighty glaciers shrinking and the snow reducing to almost nothing, Catalina knew that she needed to act to help slow global warming as much as possible. Together with 70 other young people from South America, Catalina launched a climate challenge called '1000 Actions for Change', to encourage and educate young people about easy ways to protect the planet, such as planting trees and reducing plastic use.

Catalina fell in love with science at school. After local biologists put on a workshop about amphibians, Catalina became fascinated by the animals and soon started conducting research for the scientists in local forests! For years while still at school, she counted, measured and photographed a delicate species of frog, whose population is quickly declining because of human activity. Catalina enjoys contributing towards scientific research and carries out science workshops for young children in rural areas, to share her passion and the importance of learning about the planet.

HOME

Patagonia spans across Argentina and Chile, with the Pacific Ocean on the west and the Atlantic on the east. Along with breathtaking, slow moving giant glaciers reaching out from pale blue lagoons, Catalina's region also has vast grassy plains and dense rainforest, and is home to all sorts of wildlife.

Long-lashed guanacos, a close cousin of camels and llamas, can be spotted from almost everywhere in Patagonia. The Andean condor, the largest flying bird in the world, is also native to the region – it has a white feather necklace and can live for over 70 years. From the intelligent, sandy-coloured Patagonian puma to pretty pink flamingos found on salt lakes and soda lagoons, many of the incredible animals here are now endangered because of pollution and poaching. The waters are home to unusual looking elephant seals, acrobatic dusky dolphins, four types of whale and many penguin species.

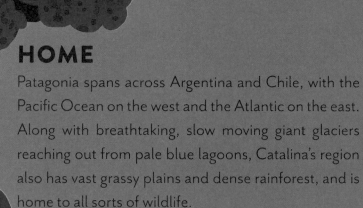

CATALINA BELIEVES THAT HUMANS SHOULD ALWAYS BE IN BALANCE WITH NATURE, AND THAT THE ENVIRONMENT IS MUCH MORE IMPORTANT THAN MONEY.

Catalina believes that humans should always be in balance with nature, and that the environment is much more important than money. Years of working to understand and conserve amphibians taught her how fragile and vulnerable the natural world can be. Even a human simply touching some types of frog is enough to contaminate and kill them, not to mention our buildings and pollution. To protect vulnerable local species, Catalina demonstrated with her community against a company who wanted to build a power plant in a local river, and after lots of hard work, they managed to stop the build, protecting the animals and their home.

CHALLENGE

Many ponds and natural spaces that were once home to a range of amphibians have been lost as humans built cities and towns, meaning that many species are now close to extinction. One of the best ways to help these important animals to survive is by creating a mini wildlife pond. It can be as small as a large washing up bowl, and is surprisingly easy to make.

Your mini pond can help frogs, toads, newts, damselflies, dragonflies, birds and more!

You will need:

- A frost-proof, non-leaking container to hold water (you could use a large sturdy bowl)
- Gravel and rocks or pebbles
- Small pond plants that love growing in water
- Help from an adult

FACT

Amphibians are animals that live on both land and water, including frogs, toads and newts. They are cold-blooded and breathe through their thin skin! They are very sensitive to pollution, and despite being found in every continent except Antarctica, are rapidly declining in number.

1 Decide where you'll place your mini-pond, and set down your container. Make sure it will receive some sunshine, but not too much bright light for the whole day.

2 Use rocks, bricks or logs around the edge to make routes for wildlife to get in and out of the pond. Think of them as stepping stones, so no animal gets stuck or can't get in.

3 Make sure your container is fully sealed and has no leak holes, then make a layer of gravel or small stones at the bottom.

4 Plant a few small native plants like pondweed and water cress (ask your local garden centre if needed), using the gravel to secure them.

5 Make sure there are a couple of larger stones in the container, and plenty lining the inside too. If the container walls are too steep or slippery, frogs and newts will find it hard to get out.

6 Time to fill the pond! Rainwater is the ideal water to use, as tap water contains too many chemicals.

Sit back and wait for local wildlife to start exploring the new pond! In the first few months you may need to clear out blanket weed or algae, but with time, the creatures that make their homes in your pond will keep it clear themselves.

Aditya Mukarji

BIO

Aditya Mukarji's home is the city of Gurugram, just south of New Delhi, on the west bank of the Yamuna river in northern India. Aditya was inspired by conversations with his mentor about the overflowing rubbish dumps in their city, and start to think about how he might help address the growing problem of single-use plastic.

One day Aditya watched a video on the internet of vets painstakingly removing a plastic straw that was stuck in the nose of a turtle. He was shocked and saddened at the turtle's ordeal, and decided to find out more about how our plastic waste ends up harming the animal kingdom.

He realised that plastic straws were really not that important or useful, as paper straws work just as well – or, even better, we can just drink from the cup! Apart from those used in medicine (like syringes and bandages), single-use plastics tend to do more harm than good, and can easily be replaced.

Aditya was thirteen years old when he set out on his own, approaching all of the restaurants, cafes and hotels he could find. Over the next eighteen months, Aditya explained to business owners that they would not have to live with the long-term consequences of their actions, instead it would be the next generation, his generation, who would suffer. He persuaded businesses to stop using straws and other plastics like takeaway boxes, cutlery and bags, and replace them with eco-friendly alternatives. To his delight, most of them embraced his ideas!

He has helped to eliminate an incredible 26 million plastic straws, along with loads more single-use plastic items in his city. Aditya is motivated by the fact that using less plastic not only reduces plastic waste in the environment, but also reduces the fossil fuels required to produce them. Aditya attends climate strikes and protests to fight for the planet with young people from around the world, and has even been invited by big companies to advise them on how to reduce their plastic waste!

HOME

Aditya's home city Gurugram lies just outside India's capital, New Delhi, one of the most densely populated cities in the world. The cities sit on a vast, flat region, interrupted only by the rolling Yamuna River and the hilly Delhi ridge, an extension of the ancient Aravalli mountain range. Torrential monsoon rains pour across the region for a few months each year, giving the area a climate that switches between dry and tropical.

The city is part of a wider area called Haryana, whose land ranges from rolling sand dunes to hilly grassland. There is lots of wildlife, from stealthy panthers to carnivorous mongoose, striking peafowls to the nilgai: the largest antelope in Asia. Rare leopards, cackling hyenas, long-horned chinkaras and cheeky rhesus monkeys all call Haryana home, as do soft-shelled turtles, prickly porcupines and striking black-bucks. In the skies you may spot a rare painted stork, noisy coucal, purple sunbird or vibrant rose-ringed parakeet.

With one of the largest populations in the world, New Delhi faces severe air pollution that impacts on its residents' breathing. As more forests are being destroyed and more cities built, more and more animals are losing their homes, which not only threatens their populations but also means they wander into cities seeking shelter. But when leopards or panthers turn up on a street after losing their home, human-animal fights can ensue.

Aditya is fighting for a better future for his country – he believes that we must all leave our world better than we found it, and that every single person has a vital role to play, however big or small it may seem.

ADITYA LIVES BY THE MOTTO;

REFUSE IF YOU CAN'T REUSE.

HE CONTINUES TO RALLY HIS CITY AGAINST POLLUTION FOR A HEALTHIER, SAFER FUTURE

CHALLENGE

Aditya has written about the many simple ways that our everyday lives can be made more eco-friendly. Small sacrifices can lead to significant changes for the earth. He believes that just as children learn to take care of their rooms and toys, so too should they learn to take care of their home, the environment.

Commit to using the phrase 'refuse if you can't reuse'. If something can't be recycled and you'll never use it again, could you simply say no? Is there a more eco-friendly alternative? As you feel yourself becoming more conscious of the things you buy, the packaging you tear off, the wrappers you open, encourage your family and friends to do the same.

SAY NO...

SAY NO to plastic bottles of shampoo and body wash – swap them for soap bars

SAY NO to plastic bags – make sure you have reusable bags with you when shopping

SAY NO to plastic water bottles – carry your own reusable bottle with you

SAY NO to cling film and plastic sandwich bags – try beeswax wrap instead

SAY NO to plastic cutlery and cups – take your own reusable ones instead

SAY NO to plastic food packaging

SAY NO to litter, and always carefully sort and recycle what you can

SAY NO to glossy wrapping paper – choose old newspaper or cloth instead

SAY NO to balloons. They don't bio-degrade and can't be recycled, and if they are released into the sky they can end up killing turtles and fish in our oceans

SAY NO to straws of course – sip from the cup or carry your own metal one

Blue Sandford

BIO

Blue Sandford grew up between two places: busy London, the capital of England, and a tiny remote island called Gometra, off the coast of Scotland. Living on a farm on the Scottish island without internet, electricity, hot water or cars, contrasted with the noise and pollution of the capital city. Her experience of life in these two very different places – a chaotic city alongside the untouched, wild countryside – gave her a unique perspective on the climate crisis. Blue developed a strong relationship with the environment, and wanted to do what she could to protect it.

Blue's father is an environmentalist who champions eco-friendly living and tries to reduce his carbon footprint as much as possible. Rather than flying, he travels from London to Gometra by bike, train, ferry, bus and finally a rowboat, to minimise his use of fossil fuels. This 853km journey takes him 13 hours!

On the island, Blue witnessed environmental threats first-hand. She saw plastic gathering on the beaches, and attended protests against the building of a cruel and toxic salmon farm with her dad. He introduced her to the Extinction Rebellion activist group, who campaign for climate action, and Blue began attending their meetings and protests.

She felt more and more frustrated at the way politicians completely ignore scientists' warnings about the threats of climate change, and realised that we are running out of time to reverse the damage and avoid catastrophe. Blue was devastated to read a UN report predicting that by 2050 five billion people will be experiencing water shortages, and felt she had no choice but to act immediately. As politicians weren't paying attention to the climate movement, Blue decided her protest needed to be drastic. She made the difficult decision to strike by withdrawing from high school, teaching herself instead. She spent the time she would have been at school campaigning for political changes, learning more about climate change and she even wrote an eco-manual for teens called *Challenge Everything*.

HOME

Gometra lies off the island of Ulva in the West of Scotland. In total it covers less than two square miles of land, and is one of the most remote places in the United Kingdom. Largely wild and uninhabited, in recent years there has been only a tiny population of around 6 people! Beyond the windswept beach at the edge, the island is mostly hilly, with purple heather carpeting the ground. The only access to Ulva is by a single bridge, and the route takes around two hours to walk.

Wildlife include the largest deer in Scotland, the antlered red deer, shy hedgehogs and sea otters. White-tailed mountain hares, Atlantic seals, frogs and butterflies also live on the island. Peregrine falcons and golden and white tailed eagles fly alongside other rare birdlife, like the storm petrel and northern diver. Common and bottlenose dolphins, minke whales, basking sharks and harbour porpoises swim in the waters.

Blue and her family have already experienced unusual weather extremes, as well as loss of animal species on Gometra. Scientists predict that rising sea levels will likely flood the low level grasslands of the island, as well as the only bridge linking it to Ulva. Blue's father has worked to declare a state of climate emergency on the island, and has labelled it as a 'hope island', in solidarity with the many other islands across the world that are already sinking because of rising sea levels. Their hope is to be completely carbon neutral by 2025, and Blue and her father continue to devote themselves to telling the world the truth about the realities of the climate emergency and to call for urgent action.

THEIR HOPE IS TO BE COMPLETELY CARBON NEUTRAL BY 2025

CHALLENGE

Gometra is unspoilt compared to many other places on earth – there are hardly any buildings or vehicles on the island. With only the land, weather, sea and wildlife around you, being there naturally increases awareness of the changes occurring in the natural world. When we are away from nature, spending most of our time indoors or in towns and cities, surrounded by buildings and cars, it becomes easier to forget about nature.

Being surrounded by nature is a privilege, and one that is often not available to many of us, like it was to Blue. But one wonderful way to bring the joy and wonder of the wild into our homes and cities is through plants. Many of us have a little outdoor space, be it a garden or space for pots on a windowsill or balcony, and introducing wildflowers provides a precious lifeline for bees, butterflies and other insects, while brightening up an area for everyone!

Seed bombs are basically just lots of seeds rolled into balls, ready to burst into bloom once planted. They were originally created by 'guerilla gardeners' to 're-wild' abandoned spaces, from grass wastelands, to road side verges to disused playgrounds. They are great fun to make and are a brilliant eco-friendly gift to give to friends and family, or to use yourself to bring life to spaces.

Seed bombs!

1 Mix together a cup of wildflower seeds with five cups of compost and three cups of clay powder or clay soil in a bowl. These can be found at most garden centres.

2 Gradually add a little water until everything sticks together.

3 Use your hands to roll the mix into little balls about 1cm across.

4 Leave the balls somewhere to dry out and harden for a day or two.

5 Once hard they are ready to be placed in soil outside or in a pot. Make sure to water frequently, and with enough light they should start to root and shoot within about three weeks!

India Logan-Riley

BIO

India Logan-Riley's home is Haumoana, located on the east coast of the North Island of New Zealand. Scientists have predicted that due to climate change and rising sea levels, India's town will soon be underwater, and so she passionately fights for the rights of her people's island home to stop this devastation.

India's community have experienced long and severe droughts in recent years, as well as raging wildfires that have forced people out of their homes. It has now become difficult to grow fruit and vegetables in the once fertile soil. Her community have always eaten a lot from the ocean and they have recently found that because the temperature of the water is rising, the fish are moving further down into the ocean to keep cool.

This has meant that in order to find fish, people have to travel much further out to sea, which can often be dangerous in small boats. But the biggest concern of all is the disappearing coastline, which is being swallowed up by crashing waves and rising seas.

India is from the Maori Indigenous community, and uses her passion and education to preserve and care for Maori cultural heritage, which has been hidden and destroyed throughout history. According to Maori tradition, humans must value the gifts that the earth gives us and protect it in return. India's concern and care for the natural world led her to found an organisation for Maori youth to fight for the earth together. Its name is 'Te Ara Whatu', inspired by the idea of 'rising up' in the Maori language.

She feels strongly about the land and natural resources like water, that have been taken without her community's permission, and believes that the wisdom and knowledge of the earth that her people have is vital in the fight against climate change. With her organisation, India campaigns for rights and resources to be given back to Indigenous groups, for them to have a real chance at protecting themselves and adapting to the environmental changes that are hitting them the hardest.

HOME

India's hometown is a small settlement in the Hawke's Bay region, located a little south of the Tukituki river, and is known as the gateway to the Cape Coast. Inland from the rugged coastline are orchards, lagoons and wetlands. The powerful waves that pound the cliffs and shingle beaches at the edge of villages along the coast threaten to make this region uninhabitable within one hundred years.

Where the Pacific Ocean meets New Zealand's North Island, little blue penguins, just over 25cm tall, and New Zealand fur seals are found along the coast. Nine different dolphin species swim and leap in the waters, including the incredibly rare, unusually small Maui dolphin. The distinctive grey Hector dolphin swim here too, alongside bottlenose, dusky and short-beaked common dolphins. The area is also home to pilot whales and orcas, both large members of the dolphin family.

Almost half of the whale species in the world are found in New Zealand, including the biggest animal on the planet; the mighty blue whale. Singing humpback whales, finless southern right whales and distinctly shaped sperm whales are some of the incredible marine mammals found here. The native flightless kiwi bird, albatrosses and the world's largest mainland gannett colony also call this region home. Other wildlife includes the unusual Tuatara reptile, and the black Tui bird with a robotic sounding song.

More than 80% of the remaining biodiversity on earth is found on the land of Indigenous communities, suggesting that their traditional way of life and connection to the earth makes them the most effective caretakers of our planet. India feels that her community knows how to live within their landscape with respect and without taking too much, and this motivates her to fight for their neglected voice and input in the climate crisis conversation.

MORE THAN 80% OF THE WORLD'S REMAINING BIODIVERSITY IS FOUND ON THE LAND OF INDIGENOUS COMMUNITIES

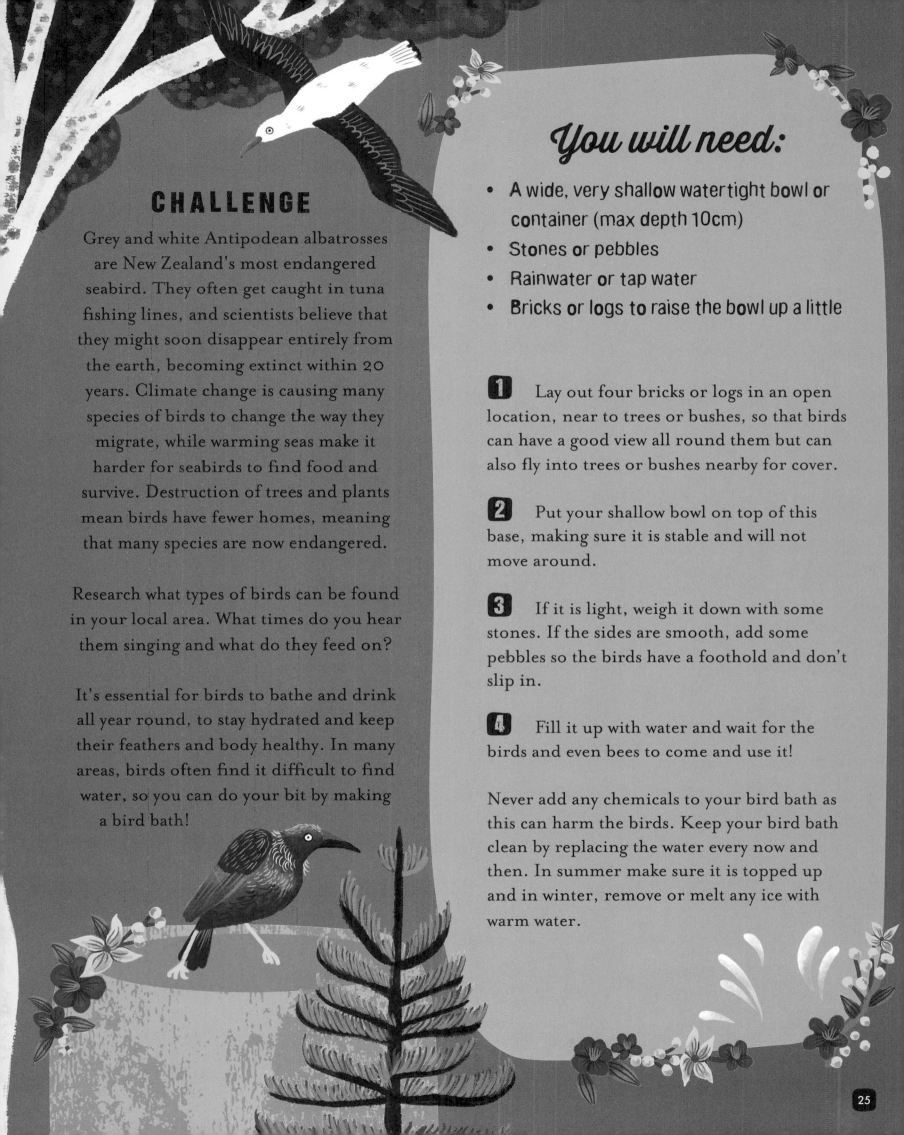

CHALLENGE

Grey and white Antipodean albatrosses are New Zealand's most endangered seabird. They often get caught in tuna fishing lines, and scientists believe that they might soon disappear entirely from the earth, becoming extinct within 20 years. Climate change is causing many species of birds to change the way they migrate, while warming seas make it harder for seabirds to find food and survive. Destruction of trees and plants mean birds have fewer homes, meaning that many species are now endangered.

Research what types of birds can be found in your local area. What times do you hear them singing and what do they feed on?

It's essential for birds to bathe and drink all year round, to stay hydrated and keep their feathers and body healthy. In many areas, birds often find it difficult to find water, so you can do your bit by making a bird bath!

You will need:

- A wide, very shallow watertight bowl or container (max depth 10cm)
- Stones or pebbles
- Rainwater or tap water
- Bricks or logs to raise the bowl up a little

1 Lay out four bricks or logs in an open location, near to trees or bushes, so that birds can have a good view all round them but can also fly into trees or bushes nearby for cover.

2 Put your shallow bowl on top of this base, making sure it is stable and will not move around.

3 If it is light, weigh it down with some stones. If the sides are smooth, add some pebbles so the birds have a foothold and don't slip in.

4 Fill it up with water and wait for the birds and even bees to come and use it!

Never add any chemicals to your bird bath as this can harm the birds. Keep your bird bath clean by replacing the water every now and then. In summer make sure it is topped up and in winter, remove or melt any ice with warm water.

Lina Yassin

BIO

Lina Yassin's home is Khartoum, the capital of Sudan, located where the Blue Nile and the White Nile rivers merge. Sudan is one of the largest countries in Africa, and also one of the driest and most desertified. Lina was fifteen years old when she witnessed the terrifying effects that climate change is already having on her country, and has been fighting for the planet ever since.

Desertification is the process of fertile land turning to desert as the soil quality reduces. It can happen as a result of climate change, deforestation, overgrazing or population growth. Desertification has been successfully reversed by people like Sarah Toumi and Yacouba Sawadogo, who use traditional farming methods and special plants to save the land.

Lina was a high school student when terrible floods swept through her region, and was devastated to see half a million people affected by the disaster. Fifty people were killed and tens of thousands of homes were destroyed. Lina volunteered to help Khartoum recover, and connecting with the people whose lives had been affected by the flooding changed her life.

After researching the crisis, Lina discovered the direct link between flooding and our changing climate – climate change makes extreme rainfall more likely, which in turn means that rivers and streams are more likely to overflow. She couldn't believe how little this huge issue was talked about, and decided to do something. At first she wrote for her school newspaper, explaining the science of the crisis and showing how everyone could help.

After lots of hard work writing, word spread and Lina's articles were published by some big publications in Sudan. Using her native language of Arabic, she creatively engaged environmental teachings from the Quran to educate her community. Muslims are commanded by God to protect and honour the earth in every way, and so Lina combined faith with science to inspire and inform people about the risks to their home. She attended UN climate conferences, delivered environmental workshops in Sudan and now works as a climate journalist, reaching people from across the world with her words.

According to scientists, rising temperatures will make Sudan completely uninhabitable during this century. Lina believes that hope for her country lies with the power of young people, and in gaining and spreading knowledge.

HOME

The busy city of Khartoum sits at the point where the White Nile flowing from Uganda and the Blue Nile flowing from Ethiopia meet. The two bodies of water merge into the main Nile, the longest river in the world, that journeys on north into Egypt, and are home to a range of important wildlife. The fearsome Nile crocodile, huge hippos, monitor lizards, herons and speedy soft-shell turtles live alongside ferocious tigerfishes and unusual lungfishes.

Sunut forest is a savannah inside the city of Khartoum that is flooded by the White Nile each year, creating a unique ecosystem. Home to troops of noisy Patas monkeys, and pink greater flamingos, hoopoes, and pelicans are just some of the wide variety of bird species found here. Conservationists work hard to protect this biodiversity hotspot from habitat loss and pollution – no easy task in the middle of a city!

Khartoum has a tropical desert climate, with vast deserts to the north and dry grasslands and savannahs to the south. The wider region is home to various species of antelope and monkey, as well as giraffes, cheetahs, leopards and lions. Sadly many of these animals have been badly affected by human activity and poaching.

The Blue Nile rises in late summer when monsoon rains arrive, sometimes causing floods in the country's capital. Sudan was hit by extreme floods in 2020, destroying the lives of thousands of people already impacted by serious droughts. Increasing desertification and competition for water has already contributed towards a deadly war in the Darfur region of Sudan, referred to as the world's first 'climate war', in which hundreds of thousands have been killed.

Parts of Africa like Sudan are extremely vulnerable to climate change, with millions of people facing starvation and conflict as a result. Lina's work raising awareness of climate change is vital in ensuring that the stories of people who are already suffering the consequences of global warming are heard, and in securing a movement to stop this. She hopes to become an environmental engineer in order to use science and technology to solve climate issues.

DESERTIFICATION IS THE PROCESS OF FERTILE LAND TURNING TO DESERT AS THE SOIL QUALITY REDUCES.

FACT

Water is the key to life —
every living thing on earth needs
water to survive and function. Our bodies
are mostly made up of water and without
it we wouldn't be able to breathe, digest
food or move our muscles. Just as around
70% of our bodies are made from water,
around 70% of the earth's surface is
covered by water, with 96%
of that water found
in the oceans.

Climate change is seriously changing
the earth's natural balance, with the UN
predicting that a staggering two thirds
of the world's population will face water
shortages by 2025. As we've seen with
Lina's home, millions of people globally
already struggle every single day.

CHALLENGE

If we're fortunate enough to have access
to clean, safe water, we should value and
respect it. Here are some simple ways to
save water:

1 Turn off the tap while you brush
your teeth and you'll save six litres of
water each minute!

2 Collect rainwater from your outdoor
space to water your plants.

3 Time your showers to less than five
minutes to save around 200,000 litres
of water a month. Leave a clock where
you can see it or sing your favourite song
twice!

4 Choose water instead of shop-
bought juice; it takes around 200 litres of
water to make a glass of orange juice.

5 Collect any water from the tap while
you wait for it to warm up or cool down
to the temperature you want. You can use
this for plants.

6 Reuse your towels for at least a
week — remember you are clean after
you shower.

Ellen-Anne

BIO

Ellen-Anne is from the Indigenous Sami people and lives in the remote, snowy village of Karesuando in North Sweden. Located above the Arctic Circle, Ellen-Anne's community have been reindeer herders for centuries, and her parents first took her to their reindeer herds when she was just two months old. Ellen-Anne loves caring for reindeer and hopes to become a herder like her mother and father when she grows up. Like all Sami children, she is connected to the culture of herding, and life with the reindeer in nature is spiritually and physically sacred.

The Arctic is warming up at double the rate of the rest of the world, threatening the Sami's ancient way of life. Ellen-Anne's community migrate with their reindeer in winter into the lowlands, and back up into the mountains in summer, but global warming has changed things. The soil and snow is getting wetter than normal, causing the ground to freeze, which prevents reindeer from eating the plants they need to live. This in turn makes it extremely difficult for the Sami to survive, as their entire life and tradition is based around the reindeer.

Ellen-Anne has seen these changes and worries for the future of her community, so along with other activists from around the world she took a petition to the UN. She was the youngest member of the group, but she bravely presented their demands for governments to take climate action. They spoke powerfully about how many countries were not delivering their promises of clean air, land, safety and healthy childhoods. Motivated by her rapidly warming, changing home, Ellen-Anne used her voice to ensure that the Sami community were heard.

Along with other Indigenous communities, the Sami's voices are often ignored by governments, and Ellen-Anne hopes that through her activism, she can change things for the better.

HOME

The Sami inhabit Sápmi land, stretching across Norway, Sweden, Finland and Russia. Ellen-Anne's home is in a vast wilderness, white with thick snow and green with lichens in the ancient forests. A land of snow-capped mountains, midnight sun, rolling tundra and sparkling clear lakes, streams and wild rivers. In some months the magical Northern Lights can be seen vibrantly turning the night sky blue and green.

You can spot bright white Arctic hares and foxes, who are almost-camouflaged in the snow, and red flying squirrels gliding through trees. Beluga whales swim in the Arctic ocean, and wolves, bears and reindeer roam the land, although all are sadly affected by the changing climate.

Sami communities have lived in the Arctic since ancient times and depend on herding, hunting and fishing to survive, all of which are important in their culture. They have immense knowledge of different types of snow and plants and are extremely resourceful, never wasting any part of the reindeer. If reindeer meat is eaten, everything from the hooves to the skins and bones is carefully saved and cleverly used.

With the warming earth, herders have to work longer hours, driving round for days on end to look for the right plants. Herds are forced to move and people struggle to provide for their families. Unprecedented heat has led to widespread forest fires, and hunting and fishing traditions have been affected, but Ellen-Anne and her community are determined to keep fighting for their ancient culture and home that has been passed on from generation to generation for thousands of years.

CHALLENGE

The Sami spend months saving and preparing reindeer hides; they scrape, soak, dry and stretch the leather by hand. They use tendons as thread and bones as tools and toys for their children. Their bags and clothes are made from the skins and they make sure that not a single bit goes to waste.

They barely produce any rubbish at all, and therefore have a very small carbon footprint compared to most of us. This resourcefulness is key in their respectful relationship with the earth and their home. Modern lifestyles are often not quite as resourceful as the Sami's, with things being bought and thrown away each day!

Work out how much 'stuff' you and your family throw away in a week. Think about how you could reduce this waste. Could you be creative and kind to the earth like the Sami, and think of how to upcycle them?

Try these upcycling ideas!

1 Next time you have overripe, mushy bananas at home, bake some sweet banana bread or turn them into a refreshing smoothie.

2 Instead of throwing away used food jars, use them as water pots for painting or decorate them and use as pen pots or storage.

3 Use empty toilet rolls and cereal boxes for arts and crafts projects.

4 Use empty egg boxes to plant seed gardens in.

5 Decorate an empty yogurt pot and cut a slit in the lid for a piggy bank.

6 Upcycle empty juice or milk cartons to make bird feeders for your garden or balcony.

Sumak Helena Gualinga

BIO

Sumak Helena Gualinga was raised in her mother's community, the Indigenous Kichwa people of Sarayaku who live deep in the Ecuadorian Amazon. Her father is Finnish and Helena regularly spends time in Finland, but when she is returning from Europe she often worries that her village in the jungle might not be there anymore. For as long as she can remember, it has been under terrible threat.

The Sarayaku land is extremely rich in oil, and many oil corporations and governments have been carelessly and violently trying to get their hands on it for decades, not caring about killing trees, animals or even humans who live there.

Helena was raised as an activist and from a very early age she took part in protests and strikes with her family. She believes that simply growing up in an Indigenous community is activism in itself, as it is a constant struggle to survive. Everyday life for young people like her involves fighting to protect her land from those who desperately want to harm it.

Helena felt disappointed by international organisations and governments' refusal to do anything at all about the greedy companies. But she used her disappointment as inspiration to launch a campaign called 'Polluters Out', which works with over 200 young activists, scientists and Indigenous communities to stop fossil fuel companies from damaging the environment. She regularly speaks up for her community to the media and at events, and alongside her activism, continues to study at school. Helena is passionate about education and speaks English, Kiwcha, Spanish, Swedish and Finnish!

Like her fellow Kiwchis, Helena has a very close bond to the natural world. She believes in the ancient concept of the 'living forest', in which humans, animals and plants live in perfect balance, without pollution and destruction, the way her ancestors have lived for centuries.

Helena treats all life as sacred and continues to fight for the protection of the rainforest and Indigenous communities, with hopes of one day being able to live a peaceful life in Sarayaku. She refers to herself as a 'daughter of the first uprising'.

HOME

Helena's home is nestled on the banks of the winding Bobonazo river, in the dense Amazon forest. The Bobonazo flows through miles and miles of lush jungle until it merges with the Amazon river in Peru, and the Sarayaku villages are so remote that you can only reach them using a canoe or a small plane!

A third of the biodiversity of the Amazon jungle is found in Ecuador, with some of the majestic trees reaching into the sky as tall as 40 metres. You can spot vibrant blue and yellow macaws, noisy parakeets and stealthy harpy eagles. Black-mantled tamarins, capybaras and quick-as-lightning jaguars roam the jungle while caimans, fresh water dolphins and more than 300 fish species rule the water. Floating between unbelievably bright exotic flowers there are 1,000 species of butterflies, and more than ten types of monkey swing through tree branches.

As you can imagine the jungle is never silent or still, and it is in this phenomenal setting that the Sarayaku people live off the land. They hunt, fish and look after the soil, physically and spiritually caring for it as it cares for them. The Sarayaku believe that the forest is sacred and has its own spirit, while the birds and water are its protectors. They live simply, with the idea that the land belongs to everyone and that it must be protected. Unfortunately, not everyone feels the same as them.

In 1996, the Argentinian Oil Company invaded without warning, attacking Kichwa people and detonating explosives in the beautiful rainforest, destroying animals, homes and sacred sites. The Sarayaku had no warning until they saw people arriving in helicopters. The Sarayaku took the company to international court, and won, but the battle is far from over, as each year there are more threats from companies who put money over everything else.

The Sarayaku have an almost non-existent carbon footprint, but along with other Indigenous communities are the hardest and fastest hit by the climate emergency. Despite having resisted and fought against climate change for decades, their home is still vulnerable.

In 2020, floods in the region swept away hundreds of homes, schools, animals and the main bridge of the village, leaving many of Helena's friends and family devastated. Helena and her friends immediately set up a fundraiser, and she vows to continue her battle.

SARAYAKU WISDOM: "FOR LAND, FOR LIFE, WE RISE."

CHALLENGE

Pause for a minute and think about all the ways you interact with our wonderful planet earth. Like the Sarayaku people, reflect on how nature nourishes you.

Find a 'sit spot'. This can be anywhere that you have access to the natural world — for example, a spot in your garden or balcony, by your favourite tree in a park or beach. Take five minutes to sit there and get to know the place, by just being present. Observe what is around you, smells, sights, breezes, warmth or coolness, the feeling of the ground beneath you. Are there any insects or birds around? After a few minutes you will not only be seeing things but sensing them too, and by returning to your sit spot at different times of day and times of year, you'll notice changes, big and small. The more time you spend within nature, the stronger your relationship with it becomes.

Wherever you go, take an extra second to notice and appreciate our planet, and remember that as the Sarayaku say, you too are a part of the wonderful ecosystem.

Litokne Kabua

BIO

Litokne Kabua's home is Ebeye island, in the string of atolls and volcanic islands that sit in the Marshall Islands. His house is only a two-minute walk away from the ocean, and he is all too aware that because of climate change, his tiny island and the others around it are literally being swallowed up. The Marshall Islands are one of the places most vulnerable to global warming on earth, a heartbreaking fact that has led Litokne to activism.

The country's islands are only around 7 feet above sea level, and scientists have predicted that as soon as 2050, they could be underwater. The beautiful chain of small islands holds the rich and beautiful culture of the Marshallese people, from unique navigation and fishing methods to ancient stories and legends. The heritage passed to Litokne from his ancestors is under immediate threat from the rising ocean.

The temperature of the sea is also rising. The spectacular coral reefs all around the islands cannot cope with the increasing heat and are bleaching and dying at an alarming rate. As corals die, so do the fish that depend on them, which makes it harder for the islanders to find food. Unbearable heat, droughts and extreme weather are constant reminders to Litokne that his home is in trouble.

Litokne reaches out to local schools, passionately explaining the issues at hand and encouraging young people to join the climate movement. He has organised beach and ocean clean-ups to remove waste that pollutes the land and water. Along with other activists, Litokne spreads word within his community by giving simple tips and guidance on how to respect the planet in everyday life. He has marched in protests, calling world leaders to act now on the climate emergency. He knows that climate change will not go away, but hopes that if everyone stands up to do their bit it can be reduced enough to save his home.

An atoll is a ring of land that surrounds a lagoon

HOME

The islands that make up Litokne's home actually sit on coral reefs on the edges of sunken volcanoes on the ocean floor! The coral reefs circle vast turquoise lagoons, and together with an island form an atoll. Halfway between Hawaii and Australia, the Marshall Islands are very remote. Dazzling crystal blue waters lap sandy beaches lined with palm trees, and the islands are often wide enough only for one central road.

The Polynesian rat lives here (and cannot be found anywhere else in the world!), and there are over 70 bird species, including long-tailed tropicbirds and albatrosses.

The ocean waters are home to an incredible array of wildlife, and the whole country has the status of being a shark sanctuary. All existing sea turtle species are found on the busy sea floor, alongside vibrant clownfish and lionfish, shoals of silvery barracudas, acrobatic mahi-mahi fish, huge tuna and powerful marlin. Long-beaked dolphins, basking sharks, tiger sharks, porpoises, blue whales, pygmy killer whales and sperm whales call the region home, along with coconut crabs, graceful manta rays and various lizard species. The reefs teem with life, home to hundreds of species of brightly coloured tropical fish, and there are over 300 types of coral in every colour of the rainbow. But sadly the entire ecosystem is now threatened.

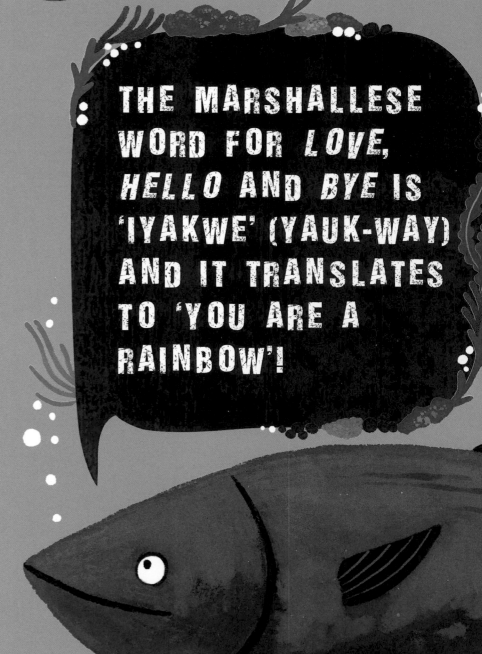

THE MARSHALLESE WORD FOR *LOVE*, *HELLO* AND *BYE* IS 'IYAKWE' (YAUK-WAY) AND IT TRANSLATES TO 'YOU ARE A RAINBOW'!

The ocean has always played a central part in the life of Marshallese people, and Litokne's family relies on it for food and to travel to their family members living on other, more remote islands. He lives on the front line of climate change, and signed a petition with other young people from around the world to the United Nations to hold countries who do not act to account.

CHALLENGE

Conventional cleaning products are very harmful to the planet, in particular to marine life. The chemicals in the products can kill fish and pollute water supplies, and buying a new bottle each time you need more creates lots of plastic waste. One way of tackling this problem is by making your own eco-friendly home cleaning products and storing them in old plastic bottles.

Here's how to make your own planet-friendly, totally natural cleaning products:

1 Put 150 grams of orange or lemon peel, 50 grams of brown sugar and 500ml of water into an old plastic bottle with a tight lid. Make sure there is some space left at the top of the bottle, close it tightly and shake well.

2 Label it with the date you mixed it up and leave to ferment in a warm, dry place, away from light, for 3 months. (Tip – if you add a teaspoon of yeast to the mix it will only need 2 months.)

3 During the first week, open the lid every day to allow the gas to escape. In the second week open it every other day. After that, you can open it once a week.

4 Strain the liquid through a muslin cloth – now you have your biodegradable, non-toxic cleaning solution!

Emaan Danish Khan

BIO

Emaan Danish Khan's home is the sprawling city of Karachi, where the warm waters of the Arabian sea meet Pakistan's shores. From a very young age, Emaan was aware of climate issues that were affecting her home, like deadly heatwaves and floods. She wished she had a magic wand to fix the planet, but she quickly learnt to use creativity to help instead! She is rarely seen without her beloved eco-friendly ragdoll named Fizza, who is perhaps Emaan's most powerful tool in fighting for the planet – Fizza is nine years old, loves the natural world and wants to fight to save it.

Story-telling is an age-old art in Pakistan. Traditionally, the magic of words woven into stories and brought to life by the teller is a big part of the culture. Emaan uses Fizza as a tool to tell imaginative and inspiring stories about the environment, engaging other young people to lead eco-friendly lifestyles. She designed a book of fictional stories written and illustrated by other children, about superheroes who help Fizza protect the planet. The exciting adventures in the stories include fighting smog and deforestation, and the book raises awareness and support for climate issues.

This project received World Wildlife Fund approval, and the money made from the book goes towards more plays and talks to raise climate awareness.

Emaan also uses her creativity to reduce waste pollution. At the beach one day she began feeling frustrated at the rubbish – mostly plastic – that was littering the golden sand and blue waters of Pakistan, posing a terrible risk to marine life. She thought back to what she'd learnt at school; reduce, reuse and recycle. She collected as many pieces of plastic and scraps of wood that she could, and took them home. Her parents set up an art lab on their roof for her and she set to work, giving the rubbish a new lease of life. She created toys, magnets, playhouses and name tags to sell online, and has been an advocate for clean beaches ever since.

SADLY, LIONS, TIGERS AND RHINOS ARE NOW EXTINCT IN PAKISTAN, DUE TO HUMAN ACTIVITY.

HOME

Karachi is the largest city in Pakistan, set on rolling coastal plains and framed by the hills of the vast Kirthar mountain range. Lush mangrove forests grow in the salty water around the coastline, and the Ras Muari coastal area has dramatic cliffs and beautiful wide beaches. The wider region is called Sindh, which has vast lakes, mountain ranges and desert as well as forests!

The Thar desert is a huge maze of sandy dunes and ridges, home to elegant chinkaras, golden lynxes and jungle cats, while dolphins and blue whales swim in the sea beside Karachi's coast. Agile ibex and mighty wild bears live in the Western mountain range, and when monsoon winds blow between July and November, green sea turtles lay their eggs on the Makran coast.

Around the Indus River Delta, crocodiles, slithering pythons and wild boars are found, along with Pakistan's most endangered species; the playful Indus River dolphin. Spotted fishing cats that were once often found slinking in and out of the river are now endangered. Sadly, lions, tigers and rhinos are now extinct in Pakistan, and it's believed that the native stealthy cheetahs may be too, making the work of conservationists, who protect and preserve animals in danger, more important now than ever before.

CHALLENGE

Most cultures around the world have folktales and myths, legends and stories that are passed from generation to generation. Sometimes they tell of epic adventures and have dramatic plots, and often they have important meanings behind them.

Find some stories or folktales from different cultures that depict the earth and the natural world. What similarities and differences are there in how the natural world is shown? Is there symbolism and meaning in the trees, oceans, mountains? Are there messages to take away?

Can you use your creativity and care for the planet to think of your own story? It could feature superheroes, animals, plants, or perhaps even you and your friends! What will the message and meaning be behind it? Will you have a key character like Fizza?

Here are some ideas for you! You could try writing:

1 An ocean adventure saving animals from lurking plastic.

2 Discovering a greedy company secretly stealing natural resources.

3 An exciting battle for the rainforest.

How can you use your story to spread awareness of the climate crisis while entertaining people? You could write and publish it as a book or as part of a newsletter for family and friends, or put on a play. Why not transform your living room into a theatre or start a story club?

Genevieve Leroux

BIO

Genevieve Leroux's hometown is San Luis Obispo. Dramatically ringed by rugged dormant volcano peaks, the city sits on the coast of California. The area is very important in the migration route of the bright orange monarch butterfly as they travel from Northern American states to Mexico for winter, and when Genevieve found out that human activity had caused their population to decline drastically, she knew she needed to protect them.

When she was nine years old, Genevieve learnt that an increase in pesticides, deforestation and climate change in California had caused the monarch butterfly population to drop by 99% in just a few years. She had always loved butterflies and was saddened at the threat of extinction for these delicate, incredible creatures. She researched ways that she could help, and discovered that during their caterpillar phase, monarchs feed solely on a plant called milkweed, and they later rely on this food when they travel hundreds of miles a day to migrate.

She began a project called Milkweed for Monarchs, and worked to provide the milkweed plant that the butterflies badly need but now struggle to find. She started in her own garden, growing milkweed from seeds, and then moved on to her school gardens. Before long, the mayor had heard about what she was doing and with the help of a biologist, Genevieve grew milkweed plants from her own garden to plant all around her city!

Genevieve also participates in a citizen science project to count and monitor the monarch population, helping with conservation and research. This involves applying a tiny light sticker to the wing of the butterfly (these do not cause any damage) with a tracking number on, and also testing the butterflies to make sure they do not have any parasites that could make them ill.

HOME

San Luis Obispo's rolling vineyards and golden hills are set against the vibrant blues of the Pacific Ocean on the West coast of the USA. The Nine Sisters ring of extinct volcanoes make a striking backdrop while the sun warms the miles of sandy beaches and spectacular bays that stretch across the region.

At the rugged white rocks outside the city, thousands of once almost extinct huge elephant seals bellow, while sea otters at Morro Bay use rocks to bang open shellfish to eat. In the warm sea waters, playful dolphins, spotted leopard sharks and blue, humpback and grey whales can be spotted as they move across the ocean.

In the grassy plains and mountains, howling coyotes, mountain lions, camouflaged lizards and tule elks are found, while Californian condors, big-beaked pelicans and long-legged herons can be spotted in the skies.

GENEVIEVE NOW HAS THE NICKNAME 'THE BUTTERFLY GIRL', AND BELIEVES THAT CHILDREN CAN MAKE THE BIGGEST DIFFERENCE OF ALL WHEN THEY APPLY THEMSELVES PASSIONATELY TO GOOD CAUSES.

Western monarch butterflies have pairs of vibrant orange wings, laced and spotted with black and white in a striking design. When it begins to get cold in the northern states, thousands of butterflies fly over 3,000 miles to San Luis Obispo where they shelter in clusters on trees, staying close together for warmth. The fluttering clouds of bright orange make an enchanting sight.

Like the butterflies, other animals and many plants in the region have been negatively affected by human activity. Raging wildfires are an increasing threat to the region, frequently getting out of control as droughts worsen and temperatures rise due to climate change. Human, animal and plant homes can be destroyed within minutes of flames reaching them, making climate activism and animal conservation more important than ever before.

When Genevieve was reading about butterflies, she learnt that they especially love bright colours. She chose a rainbow of colours in the butterfly habitat she created in her garden, purples, pinks, blues, oranges and yellows. With her parents help, she created a three-layered mini garden with milkweed, coneflower, salvia and other butterfly friendly plants. They were excited to see lots of butterflies regularly visit, as well as lizards, owls and other birds who were attracted by the burst of new life.

CHALLENGE

Find out what butterflies are native to your area, and what plants they need to survive and thrive, from caterpillar to butterfly stages. Be sure to avoid pesticide and artificial chemicals in your garden and outdoor areas, as well as choosing organic produce wherever possible, as many of these chemicals kill butterflies.

Whether you have a garden or a balcony, or even simply a window ledge, you can use your green-fingers to provide a precious butterfly haven. Choose somewhere with a reasonable amount of sunshine, as butterflies generally prefer to feed in bright sunlight. Plant a selection of native butterfly friendly plants, choosing a range of brightly coloured flowers.

Butterflies also love to rest in bright sunshine and 'puddle', which means landing in damp mud or sand to drink some water and take in important minerals. You can provide puddling spots for local butterflies by filling a small shallow container with sand, water and a pinch of salt. Add a flat stone or pebble that sticks out above the water for the butterfly to sit on, and place in bright sunshine. As the water evaporates, butterflies will find a perfect spa-type area that they can sunbathe in and drink up the nutrients they need to breed!

Kim Yu-Jin

BIO

Kim Yu-Jin's home is the busy city of Seoul, the capital city of South Korea. From the age of six, Kim's dream was to become an ecologist, someone who studies the incredible relationships between animals, plants and their environments. She was fascinated by the wonders of our planet's different ecosystems, and the relationships between the plants and animals that make them up.

Kim hopes to be able to study the rich habitats in the strip of land separating North and South Korea, but the impacts of climate change are significant there as well as in her home city. Rising temperatures have caused droughts, not only making life difficult for people and animals, but killing pine and fir trees too. Birds are now changing the way they migrate, and coral reefs, shellfish and fish in the waters around the country also face threats.

Kim was concerned at how rapidly the natural world around her was changing. Knowing that young people like her would bear the brunt of the environmental crisis, she joined a Korean youth climate organisation and helped to organise school strikes, rallying other young people to fight for our shared home. With the group, Kim met government officials and demanded more action be taken to reduce carbon emissions, but they were disappointed with the response.

They refused to give up – with food security, social justice, human rights and the beautiful natural world in mind, they took their campaign to a legal level. Kim and 18 others from her group filed a legal complaint against the South Korean government, which if successful will force leaders to make eco-friendly decisions.

HOME

Seoul has a mild climate, with warm summers and dry, cold winters. Like 70% of the country, Seoul is surrounded by a very hilly landscape. The capital city of South Korea has seven mountains, including the magnificent Bukhan mountain, which gets the name 'lungs of the city' from its lush forest.

The area of land between North and South Korea is unique because no humans have inhabited it for decades. It is this region, where nature has been left to its own devices, that Kim wants to work as an ecologist. An incredible 5,000 species of animals and plants have been found here, including fanged Siberian musk deer, striking Amur leopards, white-chested Asiatic bears, long tailed gorals and white-naped cranes. These animals are among the 100 species whose populations are threatened or endangered. The site is important for bird species, from rare red-crowned cranes to sea eagles, and many birds use the Imjin River as a stopping point on their journey as they migrate.

Other animals found in the wider region include minke whales, colourful mandarin ducks, solitary furry-pawed lynxes, marbled eels, Korean hares and wild boars.

Kim campaigns to stop fossil fuel usage in South Korea, as she believes her country has the capacity to switch to 100% renewable energy by 2050. She urges leaders to stop investing in coal, and is campaigning against the building of seven new coal power plants that are currently being planned. When the coronavirus broke out in 2020, Kim witnessed a well co-ordinated, timely and committed government approach to help tackle the health crisis. She and her peers feel frustrated that across the world, governments don't respond to the climate crisis with even a fraction of the urgency and conviction they are capable of, and she will continue to fight until they do.

KIM CAMPAIGNS TO STOP FOSSIL FUEL USAGE IN SOUTH KOREA, AS SHE BELIEVES HER COUNTRY HAS THE CAPACITY TO SWITCH TO 100% RENEWABLE ENERGY BY 2050.

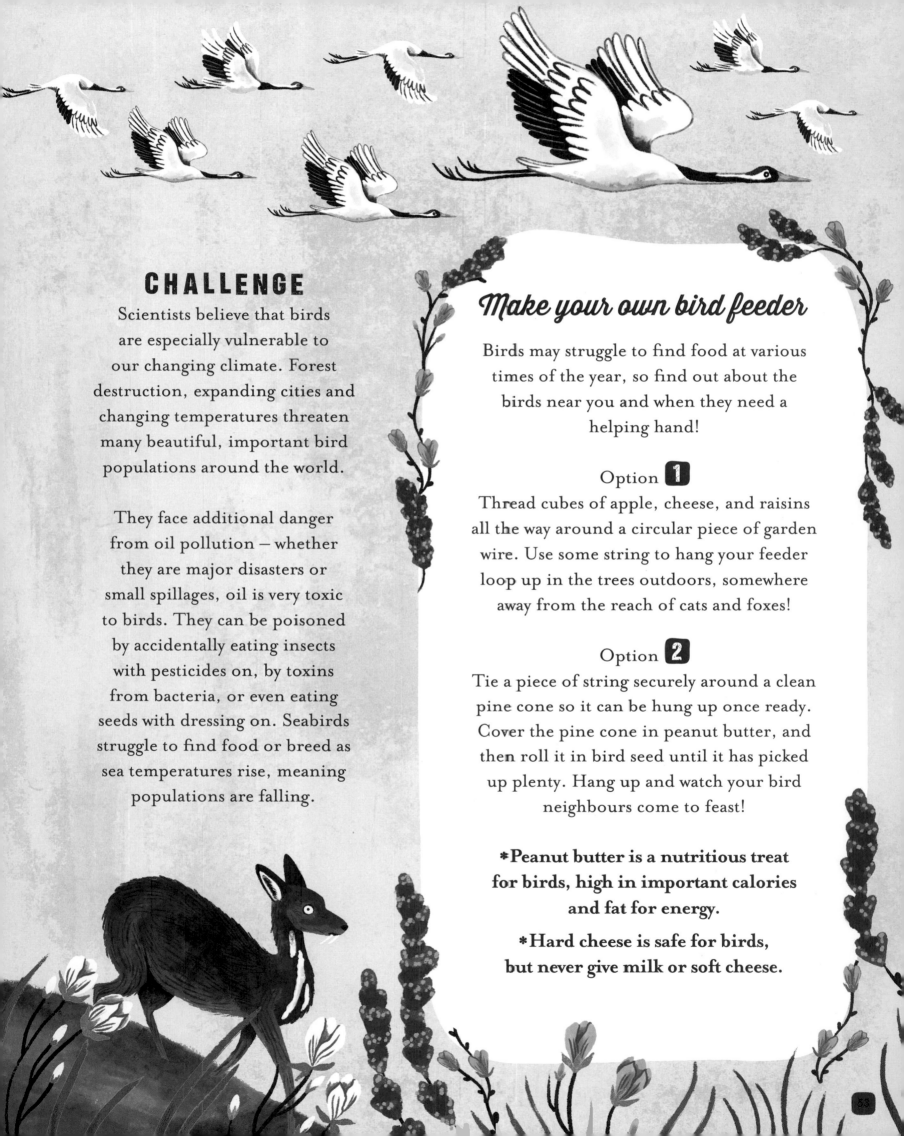

CHALLENGE

Scientists believe that birds are especially vulnerable to our changing climate. Forest destruction, expanding cities and changing temperatures threaten many beautiful, important bird populations around the world.

They face additional danger from oil pollution – whether they are major disasters or small spillages, oil is very toxic to birds. They can be poisoned by accidentally eating insects with pesticides on, by toxins from bacteria, or even eating seeds with dressing on. Seabirds struggle to find food or breed as sea temperatures rise, meaning populations are falling.

Make your own bird feeder

Birds may struggle to find food at various times of the year, so find out about the birds near you and when they need a helping hand!

Option 1

Thread cubes of apple, cheese, and raisins all the way around a circular piece of garden wire. Use some string to hang your feeder loop up in the trees outdoors, somewhere away from the reach of cats and foxes!

Option 2

Tie a piece of string securely around a clean pine cone so it can be hung up once ready. Cover the pine cone in peanut butter, and then roll it in bird seed until it has picked up plenty. Hang up and watch your bird neighbours come to feast!

*Peanut butter is a nutritious treat for birds, high in important calories and fat for energy.

*Hard cheese is safe for birds, but never give milk or soft cheese.

Remy Zahiga

BIO

Remy Zahiga's home is the town of Beni, west of the snow-capped Rwenzori mountain range, at the edge of the Ituri rainforest in the Democratic Republic of Congo (DRC). Remy and his family had to move to the city of Goma as war made their home region dangerous. After seeing injustices against people, animals and the planet, Remy decided to become a voice for the voiceless.

In January 2020 violent floods swept through the DRC, destroying homes, schools and killing many people. Remy had studied environmental sciences at university, so he knew that this flooding was due to the deforestation of the Congo rainforest. Trees are a powerful and important presence in all ecosystems, anchoring layers of soil in the ground and controlling rainfall. Without them, both floods and droughts are more likely.

Remy's home is in the Congo basin, the second largest tropical rainforest on the planet, sometimes known as 'the second lungs of the earth'. When Remy learnt that scientists predict that this incredible forest will be totally destroyed by 2100, he was motivated to fight for its preservation, despite facing risks to his safety in doing so. Remy co-founded an organisation called Green Congo Initiative to rally local communities to protect their precious rainforest. If it continues to be destroyed, millions of people who depend on it for survival will be impacted, animals will become extinct, and climate change will happen more quickly.

SAVE THE PLANET SAVE CONGO FLORA & FAUNA

Remy belongs to the Baka tribe, one of the Indigenous groups in DRC. Their ancestors lived in the forest and these tribes have a profound connection with it. Remy speaks of how the Indigenous groups are able to understand every natural event in the jungle, and advocates for their human and cultural rights, which are being stolen along with the trees.

Remy wants us to educate ourselves about what the natural world needs from us, and to try to live in harmony with every person, animal and tree. He recognises that saving the planet means saving our own lives.

HOME

Much of Remy's home region of Kivu, on the Eastern border of the country, is a land of lush rainforest teeming with life, with vast lakes and soaring volcanic mountain peaks.

The dramatic Rwenzori mountains are sometimes called 'mountains of the moon', thanks to the unearthly beauty of their rugged peaks that soar into the sky. Their slopes are home to around 70 mammal species. From majestic elephants, blue monkeys, rare leopards and harnessed bushbucks on the land and trees, to long-eared owls and vibrant white-starred robins and sunbirds in the skies, the region teems with life.

Near where Remy lives is the Virunga National Park, one of the most bio-diverse spots in the world. Perhaps its most well-known residents are the intelligent and endangered mountain gorillas, but there are also rare lions, leaping antelopes, striking okapis, huge hippos, bonobos and chimpanzees. In the wider region there are colourful Congo peacocks, white-necked picathartes, striking bongos, spotted hyenas, red river hogs, crowned monkeys and bushbabies.

Another cause close to Remy's heart is the illegal poaching of animals in the forest. The killing of rare animals for ivory or bushmeat is widespread but often not reported in the media, and so Remy fights to protect the incredible wildlife who live there. He loves all animals but his favourite is the okapi, the beautiful forest giraffe that can only be found in his country.

DRC is incredibly rich in natural resources, from wood to oil, gold to diamonds, and is heavily exploited by greedy companies. Poverty and war increase the strain on the natural environment, making Remy's work even more important.

CHALLENGE

One of the most important products for Indigenous forest tribes in Congo is honey. The tribes climb the trees in the jungles and skilfully extract honey without harming anything. But as the forests are destroyed, so too are the homes of humans and animals. Bees are dying all around the world because of human activity like habitat destruction and pesticide use. They are crucial to the world's ecosystem because of their important role in pollination of plants — a third of our food would not exist without them!

Give solitary bees near you a place to call home through this simple activity. Solitary bees make their nests alone and lay eggs in tiny tunnels, unlike honeybees who live in hives. Your bee home can provide an important nesting spot for these wonderful creatures.

You will need:

- A terracotta plant pot
- Bamboo canes, dead hollow plants or reed stems
- String and modelling clay

1 Cut the bamboo canes to a length that is around the depth of your pot. It's fine if they aren't all exactly the same length.

2 Tie the bundle of canes together using the string to keep them in a circular shape that fits into your pot.

3 Stick some modelling clay to the inside base of the pot and push your bamboo bundle into it so they stay put.

4 Find somewhere quiet outdoors, around waist or chest level, to place your bee home. Fix it horizontally so that bees can easily fly in and out of the nooks and crannies around the bamboo canes or hollow plants. Somewhere sunny and close to bee-friendly flowers and plants is perfect!

Sophia Kianni

BIO

Sophia Kianni grew up in the USA, but it was in her family's home in the city of Tehran that she first became aware of the environmental crisis. The bustling capital city of Iran is nestled at the foot of the towering Alborz mountain range, with the rolling Dasht-e-Kavir desert to its south.

Sophia was 12 years old and staying with her family in Iran when she noticed something that terrified her. She had always found comfort and beauty in the night sky, its glittering stars and changing moon, but when she looked up in Tehran she saw nothing. A thick blanket of air pollution was hiding the vast world above her. She read as much as she could about environmental issues, but she was surprised when she tried to speak to her Iranian relatives about the rising temperatures and pollution — she discovered that they were barely aware of the problems. The Iranian media were not reporting on climate issues, and most information was only available in English. Sophia was desperate to share the alarming news she'd read and so began to translate climate research information into Farsi for her relatives.

Once they were able to understand the urgency of protecting the planet, her relatives made their lifestyles more eco-friendly. Realising that many people around the world simply don't have access to information about climate change, Sophia decided to change this. She set up an organisation called Climate Cardinals, through which thousands of volunteers work to translate important climate information into over 100 languages.

Thanks to Sophia, more and more people around the world are aware of the climate crisis.

Sophia began striking for the environment in the USA too, but she was frustrated at how few politicians were listening. Ordinary protests were often ignored by the media and politicians, and so Sophia decided to do something more drastic to make them listen; she went on a hunger strike, going for days without any food. The strike got helpful media attention, and motivated Sophia to continue in her fight.

HOME

Tehran sits on the southern slopes of the magnificent snow-capped mountain range along the coast of the Caspian Sea. The range is home to Mount Damavand, not only the biggest mountain in the country but also the largest active volcano in all of Asia. The mountains prevent humidity from the sea to the north reaching the city, giving Tehran its hot, dry climate. The desert at the edge of the city means that the southern parts of Tehran are hotter and dustier than the north.

The expansive desert to the south is home to rare Asiatic cheetahs, striped hyenas, golden desert foxes, camels, lizards and nimble gazelles. The desert is characterised by its surface salt crust, which lies over marshes that resemble quicksand!

The temperature of Iran and the wider Middle Eastern region is rising at a rate of over twice the global average, and frequent droughts have nearly dried up Iran's biggest lake, Lake Urmia. Soil, water and air pollution are big problems in the country, as the bordering Alborz mountains trap a lot of smog in Tehran, making it one of the most polluted cities in the world. Sophia's hope is that if lots of people make small, positive changes, the combined effect for our planet will be huge.

Around the Alborz mountain slopes there are ibex, long-eared hedgehogs, furry Syrian brown bears and strikingly-horned bezoar (an ancestor of the domestic goat), while beady-eyed griffon vultures and majestic eagles soar above. Stealthy Persian leopards, onagers and Indian wolves are now endangered in the region due to human activity. Pink flamingos and elegant swans make their homes on the shores of the Caspian Sea, the largest body of inland water in the world.

CHALLENGE

Sophia has always had an interest in fashion, and when she became a climate activist she realised that the fashion industry has a lot to answer for when it comes to the planet. The industry is responsible for around 10% of yearly global carbon emissions, more than all aeroplane flights and shipping combined!

Most of this comes from fabric production. Polyester is actually a plastic made from oil, and it requires a huge amount of energy to create. Cotton is less polluting than polyester, but fertilisers commonly used to grow it release a harmful gas called nitrous oxide that contributes massively to global warming.

Fewer than 20% of clothes are recycled—most go straight into rubbish dumps or are burnt, both of which harm the planet. The culture of 'fast fashion', in which people buy and throw away clothes regularly, needs to change, quickly. Sophia wants us all to start making choices about how we dress that put the earth first.

Take a look at the clothes in your wardrobe. What are they made from? Where were they made? Start paying attention to how your clothes went from raw materials like oil or cotton to a shop, to your home.

1 Rethink what you really need in your wardrobe. How can changing fashions be good if they're destroying our homes in the process?

2 Instead of buying clothes brand new, try buying second hand instead. It's better for your pocket and the planet! Organise a clothes swap with your friends or school, or dig up gems at vintage or second-hand stores.

3 If your clothes wear out or tear, why not mend them yourself? Get creative and breathe new life into old outfits. You could even become the fashion designer and try making your own clothes!

4 Choose to buy from sustainable brands where possible, which keep the environment in mind. Do your research and ask questions. Choosing clothes made from organic cotton, without any fertiliser can cut carbon emissions by almost half! Buying clothes made from recycled materials is also beneficial to the planet.

Swietenia Puspa Lestari

BIO

Swietenia Puspa Lestari grew up between Jakarta, the capital city of Indonesia, and Pramuka Island, where her dad lives. Swietenia finds the most peace and happiness being in nature, especially underwater. Sadly, the happiness she finds swimming through the ocean is accompanied by fear and concern at the effects that humans are having on the colourful marine world.

When her dad first asked her to swim, Swietenia refused – all she could think about were the sharks she'd seen in films! Her dad worked as the head of a marine national park and wanted to share the underwater beauty with her, so he tried a different approach. One day he noticed Swietenia leaning over the tip of the boat, already wearing a life-jacket and goggles, looking at some coral. He knew his staff were underwater to help, and so he pushed Swietenia over board! When she stopped screaming and looked below, she was awestruck by the brightly coloured corals in all shapes and sizes and the beautiful fish darting around her, and never wanted to leave.

Swietenia became a qualified rescue scuba diver and went on to study Environmental Engineering. Eight years after her discovery of the magical reefs, she dove in areas that she had not visited in a while, and was heartbroken to see the seabed now covered in rubbish. Since then, Swietenia has found everything from beds to toy guitars, balloons to clothes dumped in rivers and the sea, and she has seen fish, birds and turtles hurt by the human waste.

Swietenia searched for an organisation she could volunteer with, but she couldn't find any. So, she and her friends started their own, called Divers Clean Action. 100 divers attended their first local clean-up event, and over the next few years it grew into thousands of volunteers preserving the oceans across different Asian countries! As well as physically clearing rubbish from the ocean, the organisation collects important scientific data and supports conservation efforts.

HOME

The republic of Indonesia consists of over seventeen thousand islands located between the Indian and Pacific oceans. Beside the equator, Indonesia's climate is humid and tropical and the country's lush rainforests and rich waters are home to an incredible range of biodiversity. Sadly, many of the Indonesian animal species are now endangered, including the mighty Javan rhino, smiling Mahakam dolphins, Sumatran tigers and orangutans.

Pramuka is the main island in the Thousand Islands cluster, close to bustling Jakarta. The islands boast dazzling crystal waters and soft white sand beaches, with spectacular underwater reefs. Indonesia has the most types of coral reef fish in the world, including striking mandarinfish and striped clownfish.

Swietenia's favourite animals are sea turtles. She grew up taking care of their eggs on beaches before helping to release them into the ocean, and she loves seeing them floating along when she is diving. One day she mistook a plastic bag in the water for a jellyfish, and realised that turtles, who eat jellyfish, make this mistake all the time. When turtles try to eat the plastic it can make them seriously ill and eventually kill them, while plastic wrapping and straws cause injuries.

Swietenia once found a beautiful mangrove forest covered in rubbish reaching over 15cm high. She noticed that most of the rubbish had come from the mainland and other countries like Australia and Thailand, and even found thirty-year-old plastic sachets still fully intact. After Swietenia and her volunteers cleaned up around 900 plastic straws on a small beach in just 30 minutes, they decided that this damage must not continue. They started a No Straw Movement, and their tireless campaign work resulted in many fast-food restaurants banning straw use altogether, and making efforts to recycle plastics.

ONE DAY SHE MISTOOK A PLASTIC BAG IN THE WATER FOR A JELLYFISH, AND REALISED THAT TURTLES MAKE THIS MISTAKE ALL THE TIME.

CHALLENGE

Swietenia has dedicated her life to protecting the beautiful ocean that she is so grateful for. Animals and plants, as well as humans, are in serious trouble if we continue polluting our waters. Our waste often ends up in the sea, 8 million tonnes of it every year to be precise! As Swietenia realised, it can travel very far, potentially harming animals and fish along the way.

Before Swietenia set up her organisation, she did ocean clean-ups by herself because she hated knowing that littered plastic bags could harm turtles. Choose an area local to you that could do with a clean-up – it could be a park, a field or even the beach or sea like Swietenia. Speak to your family and friends about why it's important to keep litter away from our planet as much as possible, and see if anyone else wants to help. You could ask to speak at a school assembly, or contact your neighbours to spread the word. Whether there are ten of you or one of you, every little helps. Even picking up one plastic bag could save an animal's life, so don't underestimate the power of your actions.

Armed with some reusable gloves and a strong bag to put the litter in, you'll be joining a global movement for the planet. If you're able to safely sort and recycle what you find then do so, but be sure to ask for the help of an adult when handling rubbish.

Yola Mgogwana

BIO

Yola Mgogwana's home is the sprawling Khayelitsha township on South Africa's Western Cape. Sat at the edge of curved bays where the Atlantic Ocean meets the southern tip of Africa, poverty and difficult living conditions in Yola's township only made her more determined to fight for the environment.

Yola has been passionate about the earth from a young age, and she and her friends always picked up litter whenever they spotted any. One day when Yola was ten, they saw a dog who was stuck in a plastic bag, frantically trying to get out. Yola and her friends were too far away to reach it but were relieved when it broke free. They knew then that they needed to do something about the pollution in their area.

Drought has also badly affected the Western Cape area, leading to a water crisis. At one point Yola and her community were only weeks away from Day Zero, which is when most of the taps would have to be turned off completely because water had run out.

Yola turned to activism to help mobilise her family, friends and community in the fight against these injustices.

She began volunteering for the Earthchild Project through her school, and now regularly collects plastic waste and other litter in her local area. She also monitors and reduces how much water and electricity her school uses, and grows organic vegetables there. Yola visits other schools and gives talks to children about environmental issues, showing them simple ways that they can help and join the movement.

Yola has since marched in an environmental strike to Cape Town's Parliament, where she gave a speech demanding eco-friendly politics in front of around 2,000 people. She believes that environmental education should be on every school curriculum, and is at her happiest when in a forest, vegetable garden or lying down on grass.

HOME

Yola's home is around 30 kilometres outside Cape Town, and is the largest single township in South Africa.

Townships were originally created by oppressive and racist governments. Non-white people were not allowed to live in Cape Town and so had to settle just outside, often without any sanitation, proper homes or resources. Nowadays, townships like Yola's are still generally poor, slum areas.

Located between Table Bay and False Bay, two large, natural sandy beaches, Khayelitsha looks out at the distinctly flat-topped Table Mountain in the distance. The area boasts plenty of wildlife, from sun-lounging dassies to the strikingly striped quagga (which was once thought to be extinct!), from beady-eyed alligators to ostriches and monkeys. The largest fur seal species, cape fur seals, play in the bays and harbours, preyed upon by great white sharks and black and white orcas. Southern right whales, Bryde's whales and humpback whales can be spotted around the coast as they migrate from the polar regions to Madagascar. Braying African penguins, the only ones found on the entire continent, can be seen cruising in the crystal clear waters of Boulders Beach, while elegant pink flamingo flocks are found around Black River.

Brightly coloured lizards lounge leisurely on the mountain slopes, while intelligent and mischievous chacma baboons often take over the roads in search of food!

Leopards, giraffes, lions and savannah elephants are native to the area, but are now generally only found in conservation parks. Huge hippos and tiny, vibrant-feathered kingfishers and sunbirds can be spotted in nature reserves in the Western Cape region.

The hundreds of thousands of people like Yola who call Khayelitsha home struggle daily with poverty as well as the impact of a changing climate and pollution. Worsened by the lack of support for homes, electricity, water and sanitation, Yola has seen the terrible impact of extreme weather changes. One day it could be very hot and the next day there could be flooding, often causing mudslides that carry away houses and make it impossible to farm the land. Yola has hope in the changes that can be made when communities come together for the planet, and stays true to her belief that we should leave the earth better than we found it.

CHALLENGE

Yola grows her own organic vegetables, preventing pesticide use while saving money, protecting her health and the planet. Did you know that you can grow new life from scraps you might normally throw into the compost heap?

1 Slice off the tip of a carrot head with about an inch of the green stem remaining. Put it in into a little dish or pot with shallow water (not covered otherwise it might rot) and some pebbles to keep it supported. Keep the cut side of the carrot top submerged in water and place in a warm spot. After around a week you'll see brand new green growth emerging! Once you see tiny roots appearing at the bottom, you can plant the carrot top in a little pot of soil so that only the greens show above the surface. You'll be able to eat the new green leaves — try putting them in a salad or making some pesto sauce with them, or leave them to grow out to end up with pretty white flowers.

2 Place old cloves of garlic and onion bulbs in a pot of moist soil. With some luck, after a few weeks green sprouts will pop up, perfect for eating in a salad or soup!

3 Wash and dry a seed from an organic avocado. Place the seed into a small saucer or glass and add fresh water until it is half covered. Keep the water topped up to this level and give it a month or so for roots to appear. Once the seed starts to split and a root pokes through, you can plant the seed just below the surface of moist soil, and you'll have your very own baby avocado plant!

Makaśa Looking Horse

BIO

Makaśa Looking Horse belongs to the Indigenous Mohawk Wolf and Lakota tribes, and lives in the Six Nations of the Grand River territory in Ontario, Canada. Her home is next to the vast Grand River, with rolling green forests and plains. Makaśa's name means 'red earth', and she inherited the responsibility of protecting the earth from her ancestors.

She was born through a traditional birthing ceremony and enjoys taking part in the Lakota tribe's Sun Dance. Many Indigenous communities seriously struggle to access clean drinking water, and are forced to boil water to make it safe, or buy bottled water. But this wasn't always the case. Makaśa learnt that one of the world's largest bottled water companies takes 4.7 million litres of water from natural springs on her nation's land, without their permission. Even though the company's actions are illegal under Canadian law, they continue to steal water from Six Nations' territory, and then sell it back to them! Makaśa was infuriated that the company make enormous profits at the expense of her community.

CLEAN WATER IS A HUMAN RIGHT

She sees this as a continuation of the violence and oppression that Indigenous people have faced for centuries, and so she began to fight for her people's water rights. Makaśa realised that in order to create change, the community must be united, and so she organised a Day of Awareness as a protest against the water company. Traditionally, they had runners to carry messages between tribes, and so Makaśa organised a five-kilometre community run, carrying the message that the water company were stealing water. She wanted to make sure that every single person in her community knew what was happening to them, and also to send a united message to the company. She even bravely handed a letter to the CEO demanding that they stop stealing her peoples' water – a basic human right.

Makaśa was invited to the UN Youth Climate Summit where she spoke for her community and gained global attention. She believes that if everyone had a respectful bond with the earth, there would be no climate crisis.

HOME

Makaśa's home is set in expansive grassy wilderness and swamp forest, with the Grand River weaving through. Ontario has over 250,000 lakes, and the name Ontario itself is from a word from an Indigenous tribal language meaning 'beautiful lake'. One fifth of the world's freshwater is located in this region, making it ironic that Indigenous communities can no longer find clean water!

There is plenty of wildlife near Makaśa's home, from the mighty broad-antlered brown moose, to alonquin and grey wolves, to coyote, to white-tailed deer. Alongside ring-tailed raccoons and minks, ring-necked pheasants, sharp-eyed eagles and whistling snapping turtles can be spotted. Huge black bears and lean lynxes live in the forests, with bright blue-spotted salamanders and coho salmon in the waters. Many of these species are sadly endangered due to climate change.

Makaśa went on to research poisonous water conditions in her area at university. Human activities such as waste, sewage, pesticide and rubbish dumping mean many natural water sources are badly polluted. Toxic metals like arsenic are now found in water, which are dangerous when humans or animals consume them, and affect entire ecosystems as well as human health. Makaśa hopes to use her studies to explore ways in which both land and water can be protected and preserved for future generations, and continues to campaign for the rights of her community to their home.

ONTARIO HAS OVER 250,000 LAKES, AND THE NAME ONTARIO ITSELF IS FROM AN INDIGENOUS WORD MEANING 'BEAUTIFUL LAKE'

CHALLENGE

Many big businesses and corporations all over the world use the earth's resources unfairly. This could involve stealing water, like in Makasa's case, or oil, or precious stones. It could be destroying forests for wood or rubber or to create space, or even harming animals for a particular product, like fur or ivory.

Many businesses carelessly pollute our planet without thinking about the consequences, releasing chemicals into the soil, rivers and oceans. For animals and plants, even the tiniest amount of pollution can cause illness or even death. Huge amounts of rubbish are dumped in the sea and on land each day, often in poorer countries, ruining the homes of humans and animals.

By placing their financial profits above our precious planet, many of the brands we may use and see around us every day have contributed towards the climate crisis. When we buy their products or pay to use a service provided by them, we allow them to continue harming our home.

Do some investigating to find out how ethical the businesses you use are. Can you find out where the ingredients in your food come from? Who made your clothes? Were they paid fairly? Have people, animals or the planet been harmed at any point? Look out for 'Fairtrade', 'Sustainably Sourced' and 'Ethically Harvested' certifications on products, and get into the habit of thinking twice before consuming. Stop and ask questions in order to make smarter choices.

Nikita Shulga

BIO

Nikita Shulga lives in the Ukrainian capital of Kiev, set across the Dnieper River, whose waters flow into the Black Sea. When he was 11 years old, he noticed that all of the food waste produced at his school went from their bins into a landfill site. Nikita had always loved the natural world and science, and decided to take action for the sake of the planet.

With his friend Sophia-Khrystyna Borysiuk, Nikita discovered that a third of Ukraine's 5,500 landfill sites were overused, and that only 6% of their country's annual 1.2 million tonnes of waste were recycled. When food is left to rot in landfill sites, it gives out a harmful gas called methane, which contributes towards global warming. The pair realised that by composting food waste instead, they could help fight climate change while making valuable natural fertiliser for the soil. Composting dramatically reduces the amount of harmful gases food waste produces.

Nikita asked if they could install a composter in their school, and was given permission, as long as they paid for it themselves. Undiscouraged, Nikita and Sophia fundraised for the composter and made enough money in just two days. They created their compost by alternating waste from the canteen with layers of fallen leaves and old grass in the composter. After just a few months and with the help of hungry worms and microorganisms, these layers of organic waste transform into a fertiliser, perfect for helping plants and trees to grow.

Word spread fast and soon other people became inspired to take action against food waste too. Children from other schools began fundraising to buy their own composters. Nikita and Sophia won a sum of money and governmental support, and have since helped to supply many more schools across Ukraine with composters. Nikita wants to work as a scientist, and to continue developing social projects to make the world a better place.

HOME

Nikita's home city is surrounded by dense green forests, and is set on a hilly landscape with a mild climate. The areas around Kiev are mostly woodland and marsh, with diverse wildlife.

Predators include grey wolves, nimble wildcats and bushy-tailed, shy martens. Huge elks, wild pigs, silver foxes and mouflons with dramatic curved horns roam the vast plains, while gophers and badgers burrow into the soil. Black and hazel grouse, owls and migrating birds like storks and wild geese are just a few of the many bird species found in the country.

Around 90km north of Kiev is the city of Chernobyl, which has been abandoned ever since a terrible nuclear disaster at a power plant in 1986. Since then, the site has surprisingly become home to lots of animal populations. Scientists have found swans, ravens, deer, elk, badgers and wolves there, as well as wild herds of the rare Przewalski's horses, that were once almost extinct!

When Nikita was first inspired to introduce composting to his school, it was not commonly practised at all in Ukraine. Even though many people around him didn't understand the importance of his idea, the knowledge that their project could reduce the size of landfill sites, while making compost to feed trees, was motivation enough. Nikita and Sophia realised the importance of establishing good environmental habits from a young age, and regularly visit schools to teach the benefits of composting as well as practical methods. Their hope is for every school in Ukraine, as well as cafes, restaurants and homes, to recycle all food waste.

Composting is when food waste decomposes naturally over time, resulting in a crumbly fertiliser full of nutrients.

NIKITA AND SOPHIA REALISED THAT BY COMPOSTING FOOD WASTE, THEY COULD HELP FIGHT CLIMATE CHANGE WHILE MAKING VALUABLE NATURAL FERTILISER FOR THE SOIL!

CHALLENGE

Create your own mini compost system that can work its magic rotting away on a shelf in your home! You'll be able to see the decomposition happening in front of you in just a few months.

You will need:

- Soil
- A glass jar with a wide top
- Organic materials like grass clippings, dirt, or old leaves
- A marker pen
- A glass of collected rainwater
- Newspaper scraps
- Kitchen scraps like oats, fruit and vegetable peels and cores

1 Put a handful of soil into your jar first, then add a little newspaper, then a layer of your food waste. Top this with some of the organic waste and then repeat the cycle again, starting with the soil, until the jar is close to full.

2 Add your glass of rainwater and close the lid. Make a couple of holes in the lid so that some air can get in, and mark where the top of your ingredients reach on the outside of the jar, before placing it somewhere light. After a couple of weeks, you'll see the contents of your jar change a little, and start to shrink down.

3 After around three months, your scraps will become compost that's full of lovely nutrients for plants! Compare the new height to the original level you marked, and give your fresh mixture to plants or trees to help their growth.

GLOSSARY

Biodiversity
The broad variety of living things that exist in one area, from plants, to animals, to microorganisms.

Carbon Emissions
The carbon dioxide that humans produce through using cars, factories, planes, etc. This carbon dioxide is harmful to the environment.

Carbon Footprint
The amount of carbon dioxide produced by a particular person, community or organisation. This carbon dioxide is harmful to the environment.

Carbon Neutral
A person, organisation or community that releases the same amount of carbon dioxide as they absorb, which protects the environment.

Climate Injustice
A term to describe how climate change can impact people and places differently. For example, Indigenous communities are often more vulnerable to climate change.

Composting
Using vegetable waste to create a natural fertiliser that will feed plants.

Conservation
The work done to protect the natural world.

Conservationist
Someone who works to protect nature.

Coral Reef
A large, colourful underwater ecosystem, home to a variety of sea life.

Deforestation
When humans cut down forests for their own gain, e.g. to make room for factories or agriculture.

Desertification
The process of land turning into desert, often as a result of climate change.

Ecosystem
All the living and non-living things in one area, including animals, plants, water, rocks, etc. An ecosystem contains a wide variety of life.

Fertiliser
A substance added to soil to help plants grow.

Fossil Fuels
Substances found in the earth which can be burnt and used for energy, although at great cost to the environment. Coal and oil are examples of fossil fuels.

Global Warming
The process of the earth getting hotter, caused by human activity such as cars, fossil fuel usage and factories. Global warming is very dangerous to natural life on earth.

Human Activity
How humans are impacting the environment (often negatively), e.g. through pollution, deforestation, fossil fuel usage.

Indigenous
The first people who lived in a given area. Indigenous communities can be found all over the world and they often practise ancient, unique cultures to look after the environment in a traditional and respectful way.

Landfill
A place where large amounts of waste is buried in the ground.

Microorganisms
Very tiny living things that are essential to life on earth. Many microorganisms can only be seen through a microscope, e.g. bacteria, mould.

Migration
A journey that animals go on to find resources such as food or water.

Organic
Food or natural materials created without using man-made chemicals like fertiliser or pesticide.

Pesticide
A chemical used to kill or prevent small animals (pests) in a particular area. Many pesticides are poisonous and are harmful to humans and the environment.

Pollination
The process through which plants reproduce. Plants need bees and other insects to make this happen.

Recycle
A way to reduce the amount of rubbish that humans create, where some items that would have been thrown away can be reused to make new products.

Rural
Areas that are not towns or cities, often countryside or farming areas.

Sanitation
Providing clean living conditions for humans, e.g. by removing rubbish and keeping water clean.

Savannah
A flat, tropical grassland, covered with grass and a few trees, often found in Africa.

Single-use Plastics
A plastic tool that humans use just once and then throw away, e.g. plastic cutlery, water bottles, bags.

Tropical
A word to describe areas near the equator that have a hot and humid climate.

Tundra
A large region with no trees, often found in cold regions.

United Nations (UN)
An international organisation that aims to promote co-operation between different countries and protect the earth and the people on it.

Upcycle
Reusing objects or material that you would have thrown away to make something new and better.

World Wildlife Fund
An international charity that aims to protect the environment.

Youth Climate Organisations
Organisations created by young people, for young people, that aim to protect the environment.

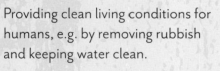

ABOUT THE AUTHOR

Hiba Noor Khan is a writer and teacher (though secretly she wants to be an explorer). She cares deeply about our planet, and is happiest when surrounded by the natural world, especially the ocean. Hiba's first published work was a poem she wrote aged seven about pollution and climate change, called 'Need or Greed?' Her books with Macmillan Children's Books include the picture book *The Little War Cat* and, for older readers, *One Home*. Passionate about sustainable development, she has implemented water and reforestation initiatives in rural Tanzania and worked on development projects with the United Nations IOM. Hiba's academic background is in science, and in 2021 she achieved a distinction in her Masters in Global Diplomacy at SOAS University of London.

ABOUT THE ILLUSTRATOR

Rachael Dean is a British children's book illustrator based on the coast near Liverpool. She creates vivid scenes and portrays lively and engaging characters throughout her work. She is inspired by nature, particularly when visiting the gorgeous national park and beach on her doorstep and when travelling to scenic places in other countries.

Rachael paints traditionally with gouache, as well as draws digitally, and she enjoys working on middle-grade fiction and picture books.